Wakefield Press

Skinning Time

Graeme Webster teaches writing craft, poetry and
narrative in the Applied Writing program at Hamilton
Senior Campus, Adelaide. He has published *The
Writer's Bench*, a writing text for students, and two
legal studies texts. In 1993 his poem *Crossline* was
commended by the judges in the *Red Earth Poetry
Awards*, and poems in this collection have been
published in *The Newcastle Herald, Quadrant,
Northern Perspective, Southerly, The Bulletin,
Southern Review,* and *The Weekend Australian.*

"I aim to write poetry on a firm narrative base, so
that even the casual reader should understand much
of the *who, what, where* and *when* of the poem after
one reading. But I aim, also, to instil in that poem
a voice all of us have heard, and an insight that
piques readers, that lures readers to return again
to the experience echoing within each poem, within
each reader. Poetry, for me, turns upon the craft of
voice, and the insight of people."

T0357930

SKINNING TIME

POEMS BY

graeme WEBSTER

Wakefield Press

Friendly Street Poets Incorporated
in association with
Wakefield Press
Box 2266
Kent Town
South Australia 5071

First Published 1996

Cover design by Kerry Argent
Book design and typesetting by Tabloid Pty Ltd, Adelaide
Printed and bound by Hyde Park Press, Adelaide

ISBN 1 86254 375 5

Friendly Street is supported by the South Australian Government through the Department for the Arts and Cultural Development.

Publication of this title was assisted by the Commonwealth Government through the Australia Council, its arts funding and advisory body.

To Pauline, Sara
and Jessica

CONTENTS

Counting ribs

I learned to count
with my index finger
rounded like a scimitar, hard
against my mother's hard ribs.
The splintered oak bedhead
had no greater hardness,
though it did adopt
the rancid odour of her breath –
she used a feeble bellow-rising
of the bones I pushed against,
sung with a wheeze
and rattle I recall
better than the music
of a dentist's drill.
As far as my hand could reach
into her nightdress
my mother had five ribs,
as many fingers had my hand.
I meant to count again
at the undertaker's chapel
but someone had sewn shut her gown.
And she didn't smell the same.

Dusting memories

I kissed my mother once
in my memory
of her eighty years
and my forty-one –
a dusty peck
rushed from a foreign impulse,
a seal on an instant
I can't explain or recall,
except that she wore an apron
of floral cloth,
tied with green straps.
We had few flowers
of any kind; less green.
We grew green algae in a swamp.
We plied green paint to kitchen walls.
All other green was really grey –
mallee leaves, horehound,
onion weed, love.
And my mother also wore
ragged pink bloomers
on her hair while she worked.

Banging the shutters

My father would wake me
by banging the shutters
with the flat of his hand,
which meant he'd easily found
all the grate ash and enough cones
to begin the morning fire;
or with his boots
stomping the corridor's long boards –
and I would leap, alert, into shorts
before he steamed through the tunnel
of my open door, but now between
his thumb and stunted farm digit
he'd twist and bang the shutters
of my ears – which meant
his fire-box mission had squibbed.
By my first school year
I'd learned the lesson inscribed
in the rituals of my father's
morning flare-ups.

Running from hell

Crisp morning air rasps the lungs
at nine kilometres. A grain of grit
lacerates the heel. Forty dunes behind,
another waits. Then home, and school.
My father says he's been to Hell
and back – real workers have. But
has he felt the gnarled fist of
an afternoon long distance race?
Months of dawn across the sand just
lightly sketched the knuckled hand.
Exams, for all the days outstretched
ahead, run toward me, too.
And night hours with integrals
and oxidation rules are stolen
orange time from batteries,
when the generator shuts down.
My father rails about a relative
in Hell, and he punctuates the point,
should he stumble to the toilet,
and find my worklight, or hear me
typing, on his return to bed.
I'm still to learn the father role.
My race run, and won, I foolishly
expected praise: my Hell declared,
No-one likes a tin pot hunter, son.

A moment at the wharf

For an hour we swam by the wharf,
diving or bombing the flat river
from the redwood piles, clambering back
to summer heat that rubbed our skin dry
in moments. Like cormorants at fish we boiled
the calm river; and she took us with the practice,
with all the patience of an old sheet of oily billabong,
buffeted by gnats and rancid slime.
And quite by chance, amidst thirty water-working
bodies, I saw a girl I'd known for fifteen years;
she had begun to climb the ladder where I rested,
vulnerable to all the heat. She hesitated,
almost smiled, almost called to me a game she knew;
bent forward, led me to her pale-freckled breasts,
came step by step toward me. Her face, canted,
turned up, struck me with brown eyes, drilled me,
until her shoulders reached my elbow on my knee;
took my gaze back with her eyes again.
She brushed me by, knowing all the world I guessed about,
and, as a dragon fly that darts through sunlight,
pauses long legged on the flat water skin,
curls its tail then takes to blue-lightning flight,
I felt love come, set lightly on the skin of my boyhood,
burn me quick, and pass on with delight.

Leaving silence

I never heard them bicker.
They were silent – or
she was – like the drop
of a five-pound note
blue upon the laminex.
I saw a red twenty,
once, but he placed it down,
and pinned it with a salt-shaker,
far across the table
from where I sat.
In fifteen years I did not hear
them argue – then I left for school,
and two days on she left home too.

The visit

Too certain, with your jaw proud,
your nose always north, and true,
with seven white face-hairs alert,
you decide, everything – just as you

shuffle feet between the traymobile
and window sill, where you air
your pants, flags of incontinence. You
grizzle of chipped trinkets from a fair

eighty-one years ago. You clatter,
in your high-song voice, debates
about the food and television
noise you won't turn down. Irate

at the drought, you lift bananas, cake
in napkins, back to your room
in your cardigan, hide a store of
quinces, pears, be safe should gloom

settle on the land again.
The apples with wrinkled skin
you pass to me, putrid in
a plastic bag wet with urine

from the towel on your chair.
Odours drip from the bag – it gleams,
pressed by your fruit. Old lady,
is it love you still expect from me?

Race accident

Behind, fog, a voice,
a reedy caw

above whirring cycle tyres
along a sheep track –
the road loose-topped
with limestone shot,
and booby-trapped with ruts –

again, the tenor caw;

damp cloud; flicking thistles
peck knees like geese,
mudguards clatter, conducted
by cold stone, slithering in seams
across the sheep-pad dust;

more jeers echo in static
cheers; unseen, but near,
riding their own cycle rattle –

faster now, try;

endless thistles, thigh high,
laced white with frost –

a comic film set –

the sheer fun

when, from behind,
a heavy wheel rubs,
locks the wheel beneath;

the cycle flips

into the polished
icy thistle pins;

the flat earth sentence
of cruel needle tools, fists
of freezing limestone balls,
school-bag, bike frame, all

wrapped in laughter
that vanishes in the cloud –

but only until
the homeward sprint

this afternoon.

Summer school

When the January sun heats the water,
tepid and free of oxygen, ankle deep
and spilled across the millet swamps,
goldfish struggle into concrete pipes
beneath the sandstone causeway.

Dorsal fins make poor snorkels.
The fish pant and gasp like kelpie dogs
trotting in the sun, until two small boys
arrive – the Cavalry. Armed with blue
flint rocks, water-polished smooth,

fitted to the palm, they slosh along
behind the fins and they club the fish –
gold, silver, all alike – and all
with little blood, compared to chooks
or rabbits. Dead or almost dead

the still-eyed fish lie on platters
of spongy couch – one slowly curls
its tail – waiting to bloat
in the sun. It takes an afternoon.
This is Summer School.

Recluse

A heavy wooden boat with oars,
found years past, caught
in redgum limbs, rubbed
and cussed by river floods,
hangs now, chained upon the swamp,
green with heat and algae.

It's not fun to stir the rancid brew,
to heave the boat along the surface gel,
to make complaints from old oars
through dry rowlocks in gunwales.

It's not fun bringing grey clay
like dust in mushroom puffs
where the oars dip against the floor
of this ribbon of simmering stuff.

But something calms me, working
the oars upon this slimy moat;
something ancient hovers near.
I take in a loose and easy feeling,
my palms, my bones, my dreams,
alone, paddling the old wooden boat.

Droving young

My career as a drover began in years
so early I once followed two hundred ewes
a mile across sand dunes, and
with each step I pondered
why the head of a lamb
flopped like a side-show toy
from the arse of a ewe.
When I showed my father the head,
we ran a dozen crossbreds
with the ewe to a standstill
against the Cyclone sheep-yard fence.
I sat upon the ewe's head,
watched a dozen crows bicker
for the nearest sheep-yard post.
The ewes drew off, yellow-eyed, hushed;
while behind my back
my father swore and hauled
on the slippery head, and a leg,
and muscles sucked and tore.
In ten minutes the lamb
thudded beyond the yard,
and the bird regatta began.
My father once claimed a bit
of droving never hurt a man.

Saturday morning discovery

Where the swamp swung back upon a clay
and sand candy-striped bay,
where ibis and ducks made parliament
with swans and pelicans, tall rushes bent
dry blades into seed prongs that nicked
my thighs. I made enough noise
to scare off brown and copper snakes,
but came quiet so not to break
the water-bird debate from cacophony;
and found a Jersey cow, silent, dribbling stringy spit,
waving horns in surprise and anger at the stillness
of her night-born calf. The mother reeled
a few steps sideways with her hind legs,
snuffed the air, and glared, bewildered
from her wasted year, her off-spring bound
for foxes in a bed of rushes, on hard ground.

The corker hole

A whale beached in the sandhole
two hundred miles from sea,
flicks flukes, drills dust inside ears,
breaks paddy melons in a calamity
of sour seeds and lemon stains
on fingertips. Even the blue car
with one stolen outsized red wheel
can survive the dust tidal wave
only because the sun snares
one blue plastic mudguard.
The sun could nearly find anything,
though, like a pinhole in a jam tin,
and a matchbox toy quickly buried
when an older brother came
bouncing his football too near,
two weeks ago – the wheels don't rust,
they're made of lead, Dad says.
That piece of plank with a knot-hole
scrapes highways along the rim
of the sandhole – see – now that the sun
has sent the whale away.

Pinchers

The Old Man pronounces words like
no other man, says he's right.
And he's got a way
with manners, too – you will
not dunk biscuits in your tea,
in my house: food's not that bad.
You're too well fed, my lad.
No coffee here; tea: bread
twice a week – the better
hi-top loaf the local baker
burns, then gives to us,
almost. I hear a bit of carbon won't
hurt. Have you swallowed crust,
burnt? Four days old?
Then he fits his thumb and finger
pinchers to my ear, twists, dunks
my head toward his thoughts,
calls it what I'll thank him for,
in years to come.

After the flood came the circus

With a fresh crease ironed
in cotton shorts, and a shirt
worn only once this week
I sat among my flood-poor
family in the circus tent.
For an extra ten shillings
each, a mat would pad our
six-inch bleacher planks.

We need all this, townsfolk said.
The tattered lion roared and glared
through cloudy eyes, and
the trainer and my mother
recognised his arthritis song.
Scruffy monkeys shrieked
and watered on the crowd
from high above the seats.

And a young lady swung
from the trapeze, rode horses
bareback, sold soft-drink warm
and pop-corn, and kept
the football coach outside just
ten minutes past the interval –
he had the next-door farm –
while the crowd laughed
and clapped the clowns.
I had never seen dwarfs before,
but we needed this, I'm sure.

Socks

At twenty-eight her mind
bulged with socks,
unknown woolly lumps
loosely shaped, each holed
in its own individual way
with toe-holds on thoughts
she could not grasp
and would not admit
aloud.

Each friend who stayed the night
turned through the drawer,
rolled among bundled pairs,
rejecting most but kneading
some he might have left
with a familiarity
that scared her.

The shininess of life

Pin-feathered magpie, swanky-walks upon
the watered lawn, curdles squawks
that sound yet of scratchy brass.
Swivel-cocks, listens to the grass,
the sweeping sprinkler clatter, or
looks me straight as if to better
judge my truthfulness. She is
far from this garden, pinned
upon a trolley-bed, drip-fed, dowsed,
half-dilated thirty – thirty – hours,
too tired but not ashamed
to cry now of pain. Needing peace
she aches to have the blockage end.
Afraid of the still and silent
muscles, of the evening puncture
by a needle that will bring a rupture
to her spine; afraid of the shifting teams
of nurses whose eyes accuse her
of pretending to make the birth.
Magpie, when you sing all night
to win a mate, keep these wet eyes,
this shininess of life, in mind.

Aunty Min

At twenty-two a black-eyed city
traveller slipped her out into his coupé
and bounced her south to Melbourne,
my mother's Aunty Min. She pressed
against him all the way from
Ballarat to Toorak Road, and in
the candle-lit diner, too.
Drank sherry, laughed too loud,
squeezed her thighs upon his hand,
her eyes afire, her words warm with
the promise of a summer sunset sky.
After leather steaks and bitter cream
on apricots, and a cordial of wines,
he tailor-made a Drum, and smoked,
and she sat for him upon the guard
above the tyre, and kept her cotton clean.
But sometime in the morning, somewhere
before first light, he clipped a pole and stalled,
and she could only fight away the arms
that held her from the torso of
her black-eyed city man. Grandpa Whilom
brought her back to Dry Creek Plains. And
now she reads the paper, tailored Drum
wafting from the corner of her lip. In
half an hour, at sixty-eight, she'll
finger out her plaits, comb the silver hair
that will fall not fully to her knees,
and then, without a word, she'll go to sleep.

My pusser mate

I keep a man so old he smiles
at puddles by the kerb, and he takes
answers to his dirty riddles from
a collie with arthritic aches.

I fling him eighty dollars in a letter
every week. He keeps a flagon, red,
and a pipe, on a table by his bed; and if
he recalls, he'll fry his sausages.

He sometimes runs his bath, forgets,
then dippers off the water to make tea.
If sunshine warms the wharf, or if not,
at four he takes the First Dog on a seat,

and, as he was trained, he shades
his eyes toward the sky-line – its just
the gulf – fixes shadows with a raider
test, calls bearings loudly if he must.

Eighteen-hundred, and he stands down.
I pass unspeaking as he sprays crumbs
to gulls. But I award him verbs and nouns,
if he shows lollies to my girls, or son.

Celebrate

Tonight, I cheer – I drink too
much. I see fireworks
exploding colour –
sky coral in the harbour.
I cry, in memory

of fireworks we lifted,
innocent, brave boys –
used dangerously. Crackers,
small pinwheels, a Chinese
torch I might have tied

to a dog's tail.
Rockets burst, flowering
emerald and copper tinsel.
Glass diamonds shatter
thunder into long echoes.

Now laws protect us
from the slack rope
of freedom. Only
the Government
can explode.

Pray this night, eyes alight
with fervent hope: God bless
the responsible, well-paid
authorities – they rule
our independence.

The ash wife

He would start by sucking
in his cheeks, his skin white
beneath his eyes, but alive –
alive with his agitating tongue.
He'd spit back into mallee coals
or onto the hearth my father
laid when we settled here.
Then wait. And I always would
succumb, and volley off
some question about a job
he'd left undone. Afterward
he'd go to bed content
with his evening. I'd sit
with cold coals, in full cold,
found now in the grate. I flick
my sleazy shawl of pine ash –
all I can make burn
since he left in May.

Funeral steps

Before the funeral I met Maxwell
cradled by the lower step
of a public bus with closed doors.
His eyes rolled, purple-bruised, blind,
two upturned mushrooms beneath
a matted scalp with lice.
I had bowled to Maxwell
in the schoolyard cricket nets,
and we'd stood at shoulders
in a Christmas choir.
But in the stairwell of the bus
white foam frosted stiff
on his stretched, voiceless lips.
Perhaps Maxwell knew I crouched
on the third step above him:
he did not smile,
though his mother called mine
the day he died.

The lighthouse

no longer calls to me by day
or night. White in sun,
and tall; by dark a light,
its wink a cool,
horizon sign. Just a
house of light – not home.

Phyllis wrote notes on label
card, while before the glass
I stretched, polished out the
hours. And she left in April
on the cream boat – a card
note spoke to me of solitude,

and school for little Gabby.
Pinned against the glass
I saw her take the sling
ride to the men below.
Not to follow – a Captain
of Marines – wilful lies.

I stir the water paradox –
a moody cod hangs among
brown moonscape rocks.
All day it waves commands,
sends crabs sideways
into weeds where lice march.

Let them all self-congratulate.
My Zen is the water mystery –
something real binds each fish.
Like cod, calm between tides,
I will slip deep along canyons
in the ocean. Life's made

of resting short, plunging
long into the dreamy deep.
Now ... now that nothing
binds me to the light.
By charm alone the glass will
cast its pleated shine tonight.

Sand sentences

Before the early winter dusk
blacks the coded shadow-bob
of felt hat, hessian coat
boots laced with leather
a clothing slop
of loose-boned ploughman
scuffing homeward,
the kiss of soles on sand
squirts percussive verse
promises – yet another
drought will kill this man.

The intruder

A bugle, a battle cry not
made by women,
sucked all young men along
to the desert beyond
skyscrapers – what need for office blocks
have people who show all their ribs? –
and you made war
more than a game
of sticks and string.
Television-grabs
between game shows
and ads for Coca-Cola
fired missiles – Scuds
and Patriots – fired
fear across our dinner plates.
We never loved each other,
though we'd talked tough
relationships, like me and Mike,
you and your sixteen-year-old friend.
I wrote notes to console a soldier.
Nothing of love but country love.
My words were to warm a frightened man.
Why, now, knock upon my life
armed with my letters of war?

Vainglorious

You strut school corridors,
your whispering tutors
supergirls, paid ransoms –
perfume, lingerie
magazine gloss
TV glitz;

you forget
mutton stew
powdered milk
apples – swollen globes
we polished on each other's shirts.

Now you wear
red pout, lashes, high cheeks,
all ripe by chance;

a year past – less – you learned
conceit, that late day-shift,
beside store-room pallets
cornflakes
a squat man
three girls at home
pressed you ten-dollar notes
his paw in your skirt
face in your bra
you counted five notes
five minutes, you thought –

alone, sixteen and one month,
you heard the glorious whispers
in silence. What beauty called?

You learned old technology
smoke and mirrors
easy, simple truths –
money –
no more hard-won
book-work promises.

Do you recall what
you once did for me?

The Jesus sect

The odds of twice meeting
Jesus were more pale than lemon
aeroplane jelly. But at Heathrow
in July, and at Tullamarine
in March, he parted the crowds,
his leading shoulder loaded
in Italian weave, weighed
beneath a leather-slung
pack he never opened.

Perhaps he knew the contents
were slight, and needed to be built
a hundred ways, a hundred times;
this demanded concentration
and faith beyond the norm.

In Melbourne sunshine, against
the glass where confused pigeons
often collided with their own images,
he arranged his hair
and halo, and his first four lines –
his baritone recitative roamed loose
beyond four-square lines
to Melbourne's good and true
supporters of faith.

He poured toward the passengers
good news of arrival;
holy thoughts of love, spontaneous
when a late summer specimen
of perfect Portsea-Toorak vintage
sandalled past – immaculate in white
lipstick – good news of arms about shoulders,
rich or poor or unemployed;
good news of revival
for those who cared
to share the good things.

Sprung against the sunlight,
he made a short shadow,
deterred only a few dozen
pigeons from pausing at the glass –
the parting crowd formed strong,
once around, or past, him.

But he knew well, soon
enough of them would doubt
themselves, and would provide,
so that the word
of Jesus could survive
very comfortably.

Developing

Across the ridge big trees
drop from sight, speed

whispers and crescendos
nearer, moan

threats to the loggers, hope
to the thin woods spared two-stroke

saws and smoke. Unseen, trees raise
neither fear nor anger with their lazy

dead limbs that ooze dead sap,
spill dead nests, grubs in the lap

of the cleared apron. The soil bristles
with saplings, mere thistles

against housing men, some shade
for merinos free yet to graze

and pray, heads low to grass. Sheep
hear the Earth, while men just pass.

Pairs

Her husband bowled all
Saturday, abandoning hours
of solitude for her to juggle
with gnarled knuckles. She felt
anger beneath her ribs, a rough
house-brick that bruised
every childhood dream she read
in discarded picture-books,
a waste, or torture, since
God had tricked her of motherhood,
and Man had robbed her
of simple things – a hand pat, a smile –
had bowled her – slowly – flat.

The marriage racket

Marriage began early
this morning – kids
shrank from my prowl
within the dish machine;
duna-heads from clattering
garden sprinklers;
from the skiffle of aerobics tunes,
sung plastic-sweet, again;
from whistling water
wetting lemon tea.
Whispering pages claimed news.
Peach slices slithered – surreal
life beached on bran.
Oats, rolled blind and mute.
Today and today and today.
Thudding doors, motors,
fumes, reversing lights, lives.

Rock memories

Perhaps in a desperate clutch
for mystery, the valley cut
right, and sealed the fate
of my visitors, who raised
endless talk of the wood –
swaggering gum trees, a good
dash of wattle, and tall
slopes of Paterson's curse, all
loaded each spring with bees
silently fixing pollen socks to their knees,
dressing mindful of nothing except
the drowsy warmth. I left
a desk and fluorescent tubes, clocks,
computers, all for this valley of rocks.
The memories of rocks, their songs
of unspoken, heartfelt wrongs
of people frantic all day to be
everything, are mystery enough for me.

The river hawk

Across the river clay and cloudy
water came a sunset hawk,
alone, armed with shrill age.

It sank in twilight, soft, ragged
grey and day-weary, cold as
the river returned to winter cold.

About the earth beneath its roost
lay skulls, white, dry signs of feasts,
the memories of my wizened friend.

It caught the crackled remnants, turned
each with a bleary eye, tasted – cruel – again
the blood of youth and strength. It cried.

No luck bears upon those who pair
and drag beyond the gentle passing
of a mate. A certain death sits fair.

Shriek saddened, I made away.
We each had but little will or need
to trap another spring at play.

Paedophile

She rubbed against praise
like a kitten in the grip
of a seductive finger – back

arched, head downcast;
her child's body curled
about each word. Her eyes

closed out real things.
Fantasies rode her down
in lilac mists and private

oblique games with rules
learned from Hollywood
moguls of sex and cash

each showing off their stars –
dreams swirled, gossamer, fragile –
emotive fairy floss, something

sweet to taste but
undefined
once past the lips.

His cologne seeped about them,
a potion, like his gift she wore undone.
His dark chocolate voice,

his fingers, made their sculpture
in the lace of her mind until she lapsed
into a piquant haze. He almost

paused: tomorrow – if she
remembered this – would
she force him to the wall?

Crossline

One boyhood dusk, when the February heat
had seeped back to the sun, I lifted
with these palms the cord, the braided nylon crossline,
to the mirror surface of the river.

Hooks, some with shrimp or flaccid worms, danced
on traces, and others, bald silver fangs,
stole with smiling barbs along the line, through the indigo
of early night and noiseless, watching water.

We made the harmony of unseen drips
and flipping callop, and bream, one or two, and
the slap of line wrenched sharp to shrug aside the
weed cut loose from the bottom of the night.

And to the surface rose a sculptured cod,
made wet, leather-mottled, and patient – rich
in years, and story-wise. His pool-eyes turned and held
to mine a weariness I almost took for fear.

I panicked, struck that he might choose to go.
My boyhood fist punched into his gills, and I hauled him
crude across the gunwale tilted low upon the mirror top.
My catch, I his catch, free from the crossline –

never free from my memory. Still he works his eye
to mine. He prickles my sleep with tolls majestic
but more subtle than any ripple from that evening
death, tonight, and he will, still worse, next year.

Weatherboard Road

I knew this street when I were ten
and it were dust – no houses then.
It could be three weeks, they took,
to truck all them weatherboards here.

They moved in Mums, with floral dresses
and handfuls of kids, and five-day Dads –
home, then gone off for a week,
changing the gauge, working on bridges.

Them was more railway families, with rules
about working, and fighting for pay, and all that –
but no-one said nothing in our town.
Not Whooper the Butcher, or Clarrie

who sold Holdens and had for years,
but not many now. Nor my Pa.
He owns the pub – with the Ganger's Bar.
He yarned with the men, and he said just nothing.

Now I come to this road like I done
all year to meet Maureen, who's eighteen,
just a year up on me. She's got a kid
who's asleep by now. It's dark

but I know me way. All year I come here –
to visit. I'm fun, Maureen says.
They're mostly gone, them women
with families. The railway's moved on.

Incident in four November starboard inner

A red globe on the bulkhead
shows dark-light – the pipe-down
call has played. And mess bunks
bolted three high in a puzzle
ease with sleeping forms.

A hand that's drunk came
pawing at the handle
on the hatch, and unfurled it
with the fury of a storm.
Half a door admits a mild

thunder of a man, beery useless,
sour with sweat and puke
and fourteen sea-lost years.
No speech can paint the clock
his fist makes in the socket

of a sailor-boy's face – and his
crow is filth, even for sea air.
The kid will awaken
in hours or days to come,
depending on the blows to

land. He might regain
his sight. The pug has still
fourteen years till suicide,
or a life-time in hell where
he shaves his only friend.

Cliff-side love

I met my love,
a girl of fifteen years,
after dark between dances,
and we made a careful
couple. Uncaught, by night or day,
our lips and fingertips were schooled
and smooth upon the body rounds.

Then, once, the sun and fossickers
of parrots on the slopes of sandstone
cliffs, adorned with eucalypts
and grevillea shrubs, walked
by and over us. The mind
can hide the body well
when one pleases the other.

But the Earth so close felt teased.
And while we loved our fun,
unafraid of baby-making,
a tremor swelled.
The earth moved. Our cradle slipped –
sand, shrubs, rocks, skirt and filmy clothes
heathen roared and plummeted, sixty feet below.

I would fling liver

Who fitted stone on stone block
high to the pitched metal roof,
to room the bed, to wall about
the table where she spread lard
sandwiches and soaked barley?
Who loved her stooped spine,
teeth stubs brown, withered shank?

Who trickled water into the dust,
and breathed on pepper-corn husks
until primitive trees wept and rubbed
against the dry-stone cottage skull?
Why make trees out here to rattle –
brush the iron sheets I peeled agape,
drawing hawks and crows to a feast?

I smile upon the fire once struck by
vandal youths to raze the skinned
pine verandah posts. Twisted shell,
no turned pebble can now describe
who thieved her Bonlac cans lidded tight
on florin coins, and rolled notes, her
hoard from distant cow-warm dawns.

I would clasp the hand that made
this solitary cottage an hour's ride
across the plains. I would praise
the mason who fitted this hive
for swarming bees, this mopoke
nesting box, into crackle-dry thistles,
into the far corner of too far away.

I would fling liver cubes and sheep eyes
to the hawks who raked their claws
down this roof. Their iron glissandi
I conjure at night to damp the shrieks
her crushed pipes released. Did the hawks
drag apart even her bones? Still, I would
fling liver, should I meet those birds.

Jack

wore sparse whiskers and a coat
patched with hemp cut from a strong
but ripped superphosphate bag.

He closed the coat across his chest
with a red button, and a twist
of shiny ten-gauge wire.

In eighty years he'd driven
two families in buggies to Horsham
shops and halls, and a pick

into coal in deep Newcastle mines.
He knew Tiger Moths and Boeing jets,
fax machines and silent, creeping floods.

He'd caught the Jersey cow
and cut her tail hair, and, armed,
he'd held it in a roll of tin

to brush acid on the solder joints
of mile on mile of two- and three-inch pipe.
Even galvanising doesn't last forever.

Dark patches growing purple large,
like mould on blighted roses,
marched across his neck and lips,

and he died, puzzled that he'd
evaded God, and untamed stallions,
and the angry slice of a frosty

morning mallee axe that nipped
his foot off at the instep –
but not the common, itchy, garden spot.

Potato head

Anatole turned ten and
the pavilion corner
where he would show his head,
a potato scrubbed
pure white with twinkling
pin-fixed pea eyes,
lips sliced from beetroot,
a carrot nose Pinocchio admired,
soggy punk rice-stick hair,
and ears halved from golden squash.

His head balanced
between a hollowed pine melon,
and an arty
lizard-grinning dill.

But he did not claim
the winning cheque
since third and second
prizes, presented first,
went to girls.

Jean

Girl or boy, we call the first born Jean.
Always have. Great-grandparent Jean sailed

to America, wrote essays in a diary, like
Scientific Proof: White Man Is More Intelligent

Than The Negro, a flowery copperplate script
my mother locked forever in a drawer, along

with medals her father won in France.
He fought Hitler's armour, and helped Jews

escape the Master Race, she said. A hammered
coin, drilled and ribbon threaded, bore her out.

Mother kept many secrets locked away in that
drawer, and in her mind. She never explained

why Chuck Berry and Elvis would damn my soul.
Well and good she didn't understand her Berlioz

or my Marx reader. My own child Jean
wouldn't understand them either. We relate

like friends, workers in the garden in spring-time.
Jean is a solid child – reliable. Today she even

brought home a newsletter from her school.
See, here: *Girls Cooperate, While Boys Compete.*

December evening solitude
at the edge of a swamp

The air sticks in the sunset, uncooled
by the jelly-calm film of the swamp,
deep, green, and guarded by gnats –
swarmed chaos, low and fearless
despite the kisses of feeding redfin.
The solemn heat-shocked gums
shimmer-paint the water-top
in thirty shades of green-black shadow.

A rat swims from a log, unfurling
a resonant train of ripples.
Two herons stalk, more wise than we.
And a cormorant plummets from
where the air is light and still sweet
away above the evening swamp,
into the gnats and fish.
And I wonder how
on my return we'll be together –
escaped from families, to clasp
with trickled hard-water showers,
the hungry blackened stove and washing copper,
thrush-tricked and remote –
after our sentences, flung in the kitchen
like wilful blankets
gripped in the teeth of a storm.

After an argument with my daughter

Redgum roots deep underground burn
blue smoke in a thread
that feathers into a ghost –
a tree my grandfather raised.
He spoke of us to come – he spoke
of my daughter, Ellie, and me.

Pioneer blood is pungent, red stuff,
hot, in the heat of work,
or a fight,
and here because hot-blooded
it didn't fit easily
into its past.

The ghost canopy soars broad
in this land. It heard the chopped
words of yesterday's brawl
that split Ellie apart from me.
But I know, watching this smoke
from roots to stars,
that she and the pioneer man
should ever they meet
could while time
silent and deep,
and I'm proud of her.

Meccano set

A strut between the pair of them
would firm things up a bit. Young
Ian's late. Why they chrome-dip
screws I don't know – shiny toys
are well enough in shops, but
real toys are tough. A young bloke
should be home before dark
or he'll take too much rope –
or she will. Too many holes
in today's metal. But that's the way
of things now, plastic, or punched
alloy stuff – rare enough, too – without
a chance. Real Meccano rusted
then cleaned up with a wire brush
and oil paint. A crane looked
worthy of a load – no chrome.
Without kids they don't need
toys that a magpie would enjoy.
And him not home again. Look
at this frail thing. It's not real.
Nothing to hold the two arms tight.

Jabber-box

I'd tell her she's pretty but
that's not all. Today
television all the time tells
her how pretty she is. Nothing
competes with the crowd
jabbering away in the corner.

What I need, what she needs
too, seeps between a woman
and man, shoulder to shoulder,
silent, dry, and hot with muscles,
field dust bogged with sweat
into the cracks of your neck,
some stooks made, hundreds
lying in the ruts of the binder,
a cut snake for interest
as the afternoon wears.

Then tell her she's pretty at night,
exhausted, your palm scratching
along her thigh in the warm dark,
and while you make up the words
her breath draws her down into sleep.

Before dawn, up with the cock
and take a handful of milkers
to the bails. She comes for the cream,
and with porridge in a few words
tell of the fox tracks near the sty,
the morning dew, the flat tyre
on the Dodge. These pass
the day-long love between a man
and woman, where prettiness
need not lift her skirts, pumped
from a jabber-box by the wall.

Ageing

Wheatfields, years drilled but soured
by markets, cared not that men
called off the plough and harvester.
Cut into quilts for hobby types,
the earth, like a fresh-swum dog
shook itself, then sprawled before the sun.

Rain that swept from hill-top clouds
bogged the soil, like tar.
A springtime serpent greenly
signed the passing of a creek.
And with a grader, gently steered,
we peeled back the soil, the silt,
to a polished pebble spine,
and we held a wall of loam and worms
about a secret, grassy spring.

River redgums with three leaves, or four,
grew acquainted in lines and clumps
like strangers meeting at a creekbed race.
Winter water patiently awaited autumn rain.
And in that summer when our youngest
swapped his slug gun for a bike with lights
I sat with you upon the porch
while wood-duck walked the evening,
redfin splashed for gnats above the dam,
and trees reached up to breathe the breeze.

Paradise

A toy elephant chiselled from ebony
reminds me of our night-landing
beside just a few lights
and our rush from the airport
between a luxurious supply
of barbed-wire barricades
and teams of dark figures
clutching machine guns.
Paradise is rare stuff.
For eleven days
we admired Buddha statues
and avoided the army
of palm-waving beggars
and diarrhoea and nits,
and the carefully guarded
despair in the villagers' eyes.

Tea ladies

Single file, with shawls cast
in startling orange, red, purple, blue,
and with cane baskets,
twenty-two women
threaded onto the slopes
green with tea.
Their fingers flashed
like scissor blades
plucking new English pounds
for their political masters.
But their wide eyes confused
some pride in their craft
and their instant stardom
in our holiday videos,
with the blush, the burn, perhaps,
of being discovered at the work
that would keep them forever
eating nothing but musty rice.

Missing you

Sunday turned on me with a square of toast.
The lounge room simmered
with downy-warm light
and magpie song.
Two claret-stained glasses waited
in their rugs of dust.
Let them stand another week
to chime my memory.
I nibbled from the toasted bread,
and longed for the honey-swimming strips
you sliced and held out to me
on Sunday mornings.

Teenage lovers

We are not lovers but mere silhouettes,
guttering shadows danced upon a screen
by desire and self-conscious egos — are we seen
like stars, mouths pressed, clothes slipped,
and enough secret parts discovered hard to
pump up the dream? And if this love survives
not quite a month, will the right stories
seep between our friends? The dialectic
of teenage love, we learn, turns about
lace sought and offered, and soft, circling lips,
and the licking flame of hope that tomorrow's
more-prized lover will forgive our confidence.

All her blood

I'll not go back to the rock where
her blood flowed,
that jagged corner of a mountain-
nose from the sea floor, to that
sneezing fire and sulphur steam.
We ran when a veil billowed,
modestly screening the sun
from the hurtle of uncles and women,
her sisters and mother,
away, away, but in fearful circles,
not far enough from the whipping serpent rock,
evil stuff that wriggled and licked as no rock should do,
out on a snorting, sucking lava burn.
I saw how flesh melts, flares, and no proof remains.
Huts, too, melt away, in the river of rock.
And uncles, sisters, mother – all her blood.
So quick, so quick – but I can still see their eyes.
I'll not go back.

Down Bulmer Lane

I wear a cane in me hand –
as if me billowing coat,
a gift from a Salvo girl in exchange
for a grunt in me throat,
did not sign clearly enough
I am old.
And me pizzle's flat,
so me pants is damp.
I make me three-masted way
down Bulmer Lane,
by the Bulmer Arms, where by now,
as I say by the moon,
the chef's mate has scraped the plates
into bins in the lane. I'll feast
on cabbage sog left by fat little boys
and girls, going Chinese for the night.
If I've timed it right I'll sail
me three-masted gait straight through
the shadows where, the devil knows,
surprises wait –
stormy drunks and young 'uns,
who years ago took me watch,
and numerous coats,
and me Thursday cheque.
I watch the shadows, and if they move,
I sigh, and brace meself for the storm.

Skinning time

Pinch the skin tight, just
below the knee, and with
a wristy jerk you can strip
flesh bare to the crotch.
Do the other side, then rip
the coat away to the neck,
a tube pulled fur inward.
Nick the neck, there, tug, and
presto, a skin to dry, stew
meat for the pot, the gut and
liver for dogs – the cats chew
the heads. That white, fatty
stuff is milk. This is a doe.
For old bucks you need
the knife to break in. And
if my Old Man calls me
Shit Useless once again
in front of Julie Zadow, or
my footy coach, I'll draw
the dirk under his jaw, all
the way from ear to ear,
just you wait and see.

The plate dance

With a pious, awful calm, two plates grind forward,
one low, about the other's throat,
the high plate content
to mash the lower skull.
They have beauty. Entwined lovers grind so.
They distract us from their dark, secluded coupling
with an icy ribbon.

Circled from above,
the glacial flag is seen to flick –
pink-purple colours, bruised hues, pastel sheens.
Unfurled beneath the sun
the ribbon cracks, and ice-cliffs fall and heave.

Listen – glacial crackle:
rock-splitting scrapes;
and sometime rim-shot rifle snaps.
Shiver to the snow wind obbligato.
And that basso voice – unseen, with vibrato
traced only through secret
ice-clawed bones of plates that dance.

That voice I know.
It is an old and weary, stubborn moan,
felt, and rarely heard. I grip that grinding pulse
with all my frame, day-long-day-long-day.
It tilts my home.

I hope I die before my family dance is done,
one plate high, one buried.
But all around I hear the dance song sound.

Liver hands

I can age a man by the liver of his skin,
and my father had aged fast
since I met Marie.
She had turned him over – skinned him.
He did not smile, or nod praise – he gave
nothing of himself should my bike slip its chain.
How can a pretty girl bring liver to the hands
by the way she swings her leg
across the arm of a lounge chair?
Just last year those hands held out
to me a small beer bottle,
and today they held a sudden cuff
that nearly spilled the ice
from my Southern Comfort glass.
Once, beneath Micky's low billiard table lights
I glimpsed liver skin loose-looped
about an ageing arm,
and I smiled, sour –
it rings through my family.

The dancing girl

It soon will turn to midnight.

You unzip your dress
and stage your legs
at table height – two hundred
men and women suck their
breath, while the sheen of sweat
licks about your brow, plastic face.
A felt hat leaves an old man bald,
fans your saline breasts –
not like any girl's I've seen, but
I'd heard the metal choruses
upstairs, yesterday; your voice
pitched at mother's scorching treble.

You high-kick the scarlet dress
beyond our family table – all
sit thunder-dumb. Four hundred
eyes peer through the film
of your pretence at elegance and skill.

I can't see you, even now,
without your voice making words
to free me from our mother's steel
interrogation, my night of liberty
two summers gone. You holidayed,
home from Melbourne, with polished lies –
I loved you then. But where
were you, that you needed
to be with me that night, and, sister –
should I call you sister,
still? – where are now, while
your body weaves upon the table stage?

The braying of a cow

I have hidden in the hollow of a down-filled mattress
while all the air wallowed in white cloud,
and all the warmth that came upon the morning
wrapped itself within the braying of a cow
divided from its stillborn calf.
Even with my eyes screwed shut
I could see the wracked, plaintiff voice
make a hoarse and bloody spray into the woolly cold.
All night it launched its song, the cow.
And comfort and confusion returned
upon the heavy dawn echo
of a lonely cow's braying
bounced sharp upon the Murray River wall.

Surface life

A boy wandered on the narrow pad
macadamised by sheep among weightless thistles
and white stone marble-rollers. No dust,
no sandalwood or mallee trees, no top soil here.
A goshawk, brown against the sun and sometimes
sharp shriek loud, steered his boots
across the limestone crust.
High piled cushions did not damp
the goshawk's cry, did not dull
the shadow spilled upon the child,
who could not find the airy rungs
every fledgling goshawk knows.

Shadow life

An evening shadow wandered from a sugar gum
into the breaking pen, where I waited
for a sign. Perhaps it came,
smuggled in the wrap of ageing light –
a spider, with one white stripe
upon its grey tunic, dropped
from the snubbing post,
abseiling soft into the margins of my sight.
With such skill, spider, why
have you but one stripe?
Does your blaze notch up years?
I chalked up half a hundred with my wife,
yet I suck my tea, and she dusted
clean onion jars to kill the nights.
Beneath a weeping pepper tree hangs a pipe
she rang when she'd slapped potato mash,
and corned beef, upon a plate:
her art could not be found in pickled meat.
The pipe swings still, listening for her step.
But tonight she lies quiet. Ah,
Spider, do you dangle from the thread
to hear the end of your solitary plight?

Black swan

Buffalo Bill never sprayed a black swan
with lead pellets fed from a 12-gauge shell
until a bouquet of pulped bones and flesh
flowered on an algae-dusted ox-bow lake.
When the carcass caught in bull-reeds
at the water's edge, flies, then maggots,
drilled and made a swan-meat city.
The dirty six-day death
billowed in the reeds like a velvet spinnaker.
The killing pleased the flies,
and yabbies, and an armada
of shrimp – delicate translucent
vacuum cleaners with pretty table manners.
Perhaps swamp-water carp ate maggots
when they slipped from the shrinking
swan meat, but that's not good.
I'd rather carp starved.
Buffalo Bill shot bison that never charged a man,
but he did not shoot a black swan.

Beneath clouds

Nothing cuts noble, clear shapes
in dam water – the mirror skin
knits passing clouds
into shrewd pewter ghosts;
ancient tails stir clay atoms
into suspended mail: in the day's light,
from the bottomless heart of the dam,
nothing but shadows decidedly show.

Two braided hairs rise
through the grey water film, lie slack,
looped like miniature round-leather
stockwhips on scarred, sterile ground.

A boy,

     raised to suck dark berry-blood
beside plump little starlings, to scare-skelter
rabbits from tussocks to shrubs,
to clip scampering plovers with pellets or darts,

nursed close to clay ooze and loose sand,
to read the bones and claws of centuries
called by cliffs with hoarse memories,

dared to pit skin against pinchers –

a foraging yabby, a lone child at play,
and the slow making of murky clouds:
two predators forgetting what time will say.

Potholes

swirl and loop
toward the Honda's glowing eye –
fast balls to rip me out
of the quilted vinyl seat.
The December night unfolds both
a basepath of bitumen from its
dark diamond of surprise,
and these rubble pots, hard pitched.
My play may bring
a score, a run to home,
away across the blackened plains;
or an out, rolled beneath a diesel truck,
or tossed across a boundary fence,
a body slung to drip and cure alone,
until the morning crows arrive.

Before the net

A net, white nylon cord patched
into squares, a fabric of edges,
the margins of holes,
soars to the C-channel girders,
binding the roof to the four
hundred students spread in rows
at exam desks. Even rows have holes.
Balloons, flat from a party,
or some athletic plan,
dangle in pairs, trapped in the mesh,
blue and red bags deflated –
all energy, all life banished
to hide in the warm gym air.
Wearing white blouses, or
green and tight show-me-off shirts –
leaving boys confused
in baseball caps with Celtic's logos –
candidates calculate Biology
success. Some scribble,
pressing out urgent, fervent answers;
some jot notes, and swig water
while monitoring friends down the row;
some pick at hair stranded, beached
on their blouses, or they fan baseball
caps in fatigued or lazy semaphore,
gestures toward exam success.
Time leaks away, and like balloons,
too many souls deflate, snared in the net
cast to catch drifters, dreamers,
and desperately different people.

Starting over

Tonight we must spread the tablecloth soft,
smooth, a cloud landed
clear of the crackle of charge
escaping to Earth. Tonight
we must hold the long stemmed glasses
and sip Chardonnay, and talk only
of Lieu, sprawled asleep in the railed cot.
Together we must scrape off
remnants of chicken, corn cobs,
and yesterdays, and sit entwined,
soothed by the smatter of news and story
danced by the television screen.
For if we dwell on the bundle,
sunk in veneered oak,
if we count the unfolded rugs,
some new, after Ellis tumbled,
change-table to arrow-sharp corner
of a pulled nursery drawer,
tomorrow we'll hunt
each other with dogs.

Searching for a stone

The rump of Arnie S. rolls
and shudders in grey suit trousers,
stained with fresh cooking grease.
His haunches swing
the coat vent, as if that
rhythm would decoy
the likes of me.
I'll find two rocks,
and skip one from his shoulder,
that his face will turn
to kiss the second square and cold.
He plods, alone – Jane fled,
hurrying kids and clothes
from their cringing house.
Last week the daughter
of our young postmaster told
how Arnie S. stopped her bicycle
in the twilight of Nineteenth July.
There – I see a baseball
of a rock. Now, one more.

Stepping on

I can't wrap my tongue clean
about the vowels of love
when you wring tears from me.
My child, a little joy
seeps into my bones
when you glide from racks of frocks
to blouses bundled in battalions.
But you weigh cloth too quickly –
as you scale a mother's love.
You claim a little learning
is only dangerous. And I
spent just a few years within
the walls of schools. But
I have dined on tall bread
topped with carbon crust –
such bread you've not seen.
I've kept off rain with a wheat sack,
wired about my throat.
And the glassy slivers
of blocked feeding-ducts
have twisted deep and gouged my chest.
But come – Miss Designer Jeans, Miss
Perfumed Art – let us fight – and part
to draw on the time when we again
can talk, of chicken pox and buttons,
and we can once more show our love.

Making it new

Chantal, don't spit on me
those tart pips of advice
learned by your father
on frost-mute mornings,
wood-cutting a whole day
apart from people.
He whittled those words
without an audience or union
to applaud his field-born thoughts.
Perhaps even he would not agree
with himself today. But you
echo the ice of his life,
and you forget the thick, clear skin,
gathered in pads below his fingers.
He knew how the axe gripped him.
My girl, you strop wit
on a belt drawn tight by fashion,
not on the strap buckled to mark off hips
from the dark and salty singlet, and bold ribs.

Nightfire

Orange remnants still seared the sky.
The night dropped black upon our empty faces,
and the glaze of unseen heat shook on.
Beyond the ridge the seething bush
crackled with exploding eucalyptus trees.
We sent Adam off to watch
the shaggy monster prowl the dark –
he might stay awake another hour,
since was proud. We four
turned to bed.

But the peace of death was foiled
by a grey kangaroo,
irritable from raw welts
scorched along its haunches.
Upon the homestead lawn
it waited, exhausted
by the dragon, and its contempt
for the tree of man.

Elegy

Marguerite Blaise A., your secret I guard –
I cannot even whisper how your tendons sang,
your knuckles, your fingers, turned
like wild-flowers toward the sun – they
pointed at years passed
in searing arthritic symphony: you wore
an unkempt bunch of talons,
bereft of strength and the prettiness of hands.

You strayed young upon that stage,
an untrained actor without the props
or script to make life's humour,
where young women's pain
was childbirth, this other stuff unknown –
and all your talents withered in a rush
of forty years in mute torture.

But you may rest today, for I
cannot say your secret,
how you breathed your pain.

Home bound

She swayed along the track, weighed
beneath a hemp bag – fruit and flour.
And two flagons. She billowed
with cauliflower, Ruth said,
left by the older son. Still she
could fight off the younger cockerel
with a handful of scissors. And she must.
Her breath knocked about her chest
in callous blows.
Ruth, at least, tingling and quilted warm,
could not see her climb off to the cottage
where she cooked and folded
to the woodcutter, and his feral sons.
But each step ripped the satin touch, the wrap
Ruthie draped across her arms and breasts.
Where now, my sweet Ruth? Where? – only
to prepare for the rough skin
and sour breath of dark. Only that.
At night upon the timbered slopes
she sobbed in harmony with mopokes.
And then she'd grasp the dynamite
of sleep, loaded with exploding dreams.
She rested at the bridge, and sighed,
and watched the morning trout
fire glass spray across the creek.

On seeking to dismiss an ageing teacher

His guile flashed from pupils that shrank
into slits, squinting not at the light,
but into the beam of our steely gaze.
He sniffed, loud, his upper lip curled – and he set
old, dry logs, and stone, into a wall
against our cry, our one-moulded mind
that half-accused him,
that claimed he was buttoned against
our candy-floss army – and he
cartwheeled knuckle-bones over our plans:
Promises; Doubts; Allegations, and Blame.
And so he stays, parading the grim calm
and stealth of a caged copper-head,
always turning, always licking the air,
all the while washing
their minds with vinegar.

The dancer

I have been privileged to dance
with a man within a sacred place,
where the beauty of his lift
and turn inspired me, and all who watched.
He brought his body forward
with short steps, foot
on foot picked low and stamped soft
with the grace, the weightless guile,
of a wary desert stalker come to hostile water.
He stood erect, at intervals,
as if detecting danger.
On a mission in a foreign land,
his brown eyes flickered
upon each obelisk of strange, important customs.
He danced his head on angles,
subtle tilts that held his cheeks adjacent,
but kept opposite, to vital elements
that rubbed his body soft, a friction
for the story he would tell:
it charged his thigh, turned inward, outward,
pushed on, then swung and swayed
upon by hips and torso —
the maestro at his dance.
He made his body listen
to an instrument that hummed
and throbbed breathlessly,
and he kept the rhythmic drone
while he told an ancient hunger
rite made clear to us
with palms and brow and thighs

for consonants and vowels.
He moved upon a carpet
kept spotless for the dance,
and he used with silent power
ancient learning of
the falling light and shade,
found here in discrete
fluorescent tubes.
His dialogue with pens
chained upon the desk held
me speechless.
Even though he did not touch
them, he worked their shafts
with his eyes across the space.
And as a crisis in his dance,
as a climax, he circled, spiralled,
even froze, one foot
raised, in a movement that crescendoed
energy for the want of it,
about a vital form
ruled and printed candidly
in black on white.
I watched, awed, almost
breathless too, my partner in our dance,
before he knew all there was to know
about the chasm that he sensed,
and he faded back into the sunlight,
into bitumen and dust,
into numbers pummelled numb by a machine.

To a child leaving home

Three simple keys, two bronze,
and one of chrome, held –
trapped, you claim –
by an imperfect ring, a circle
split at once to hold yet fold
to the will of fumbling fingers:
these unlatch our door.

Locked, alarm armed, this house
opens like the ring for keys
when you merely reach. The walls tower
against the wind, but each brick
pivots on its mortar joint, agape to
let you breathe. Home is not jail.
Where you wander, there we wander too.

I cannot love you more than
to open every seam of this house
and each clasp and latch, to set you
free to roam, and to beckon you to
warmth and light when you ache, cold, alone
and travel worn. Daughter, fly –
slip free your key, and soon turn this lock undone.

Home-coming

She held Summer at Eighteen,
brass-framed, the stranger beside her
in this garden pose, snapped, frozen at
the formal "Do" Ladies did with tomato
and cucumber salad, this far out.
She felt his chuckle vibrate
through her gloves –
a solid peal, thick,
eased from lips not
painted in a studio, from
a throat, polished yet too thick,
and slipped into a collared shirt
by a bizarre but brilliant artist.
His eyes dragged her across the years,
the pull of chance,
a tide that ebbs once only,
she knew, now.
He'd be ... thirty-seven.
Children.
She sipped white rum,
cursed silently, to chide herself
for opening the envelope,
the capsule of all this ... time
before she'd unfurled her dreams
and leaned toward the bracelet
of a starlet, dangled out of reach,
just beyond the ashtray.

Coming away

We met in Gosford, and swooped
north along the highway, naming thirty
women Sweetheart when we crashed
at dusk in bars and dining rooms.
Baxter fuelled the Harleys with a jemmy
bar and hose, plied to idle cars while
I studied hard the blistered signs
along the streets. For two weeks
I turned and worked in asphalt,
protected from the thieves' itch
by a petrol-driven earth-quake
I'd agreed to ride. Summer snarled,
drove off the fledgling Spring.
I burned raw, and pulled out early
for the hotel room where I hid my council pay.
Had Baxter read my mind? – he lay
straddled on my bed beside a school-kid
wearing lipstick and herpes, and bruises
on her wrists. But he was there for me.
I thundered out toward the hinterland,
and returned to a waterfall we knew,
where wise lizards calibrated energy
seeping from the rocks. I dozed, and stirred
to find a cloud aflame, blazing orange
until night-fall drowned the sun.
Baxter's Harley growled and purred along
the switchback gorge, and I stretched
peeling biceps, and kicked at gravel
nipples in the rubble of a settler's home.

I ambushed him beside the crumbled hearth.
Blue evening light showed the girl – barefoot,
hiked uniform unbuttoned on a pointed breast –
when to scream while we gouged, kneed,
jabbed – I could, too. I did.
The night-time held its dark pistol
of surprise to all our temples: we three,
little girl, have a long way each to go.
I rode out soon, my lip numb and bloated
where he'd ripped it with his teeth.
And, heading south, near Gladstone,
I wondered if he'd even care
to take the girl back into town.

At washing up

On Thursday at the kitchen sink
Sybil dropped a plate. Aged china
sprayed the rubber tiles as jagged junk.
The Old Man's oaths came more regular
than rain, and Sybil weren't surprised.
Nor by the cuff of his knuckles,
crazed, armour-callused weapons
he also used for work. Her head
knocked across the Besser-blocks
into the door that led to nowhere.

Her temple split and leaked
onto a calico bag
filled with loops of twine
and cord awaiting usefulness.
Sybil found the broom behind the door,
and, soon, a rag to pat blood.
My father returned to his Chronicle,
parenting done. Mother's eyes
touched the wound, measuring,
but silent. Her breath sucked sharp
through twists of lips – she had loud,
scratching fingers. And she sometimes
uttered scoffs that startled visitors,
who never called again.

Nor did I speak. Too clear
I heard the echoes of his morning
bawl – barked commands.
He'd rattled at my school bike
like a starving feral cat, deposited
and stoked inside a wire fish-cage.
And I, beside the tyre,
punctured by a thorn,
received his volley in the manner
of a work dog,
blamed for an open gate.

And I didn't tell him then,
or now, of last Saturday at dusk,
when I'd pulled yabbies from the swamp,
and he'd walked upon the river bank
and turned to cross the pipeline,
trestled high, and black with tar,
when he'd quivered at the fury
of a puff of sunset breeze,
and with a drop of several metres
to the surface of the water,
how he'd knelt and baby-crawled –
not hidden, or unwatched, as he'd have liked.

Watching whales

Each day the whales rolled
through clipper-ridden swell,
reached high to tilt and smack
the rays of infant spring.

How calm and sure they stirred
the wool of hanging wind,
blue and warm, thick draped
bolls, halos jewelled with spray.

Eagles, brown on sandstone
pews, forgave the hunt,
dreamed the days, bleary-eyed
in sunny awe and silence.

From these cliffs I shared
the heart-beat of a whale-bull,
tip-touched and sung
upon by southern belles.

And so the sodden air of whales
bathed me late and slow;
wished your tongue-tip torch
me raw once more before I go.

In the killing pen

Martha Kroehn returned from school when heat
and sweat returned to overwhelm the spring.
Hobbled in my acne days,
two years then were each a mile long.
I didn't see her hair – nutty brown, my mother said –
until later, in the shearing shed.
But she'd changed – I knew it from her smell.
Not a trace of lavender wash, or brittle
sprayed-on hair fix, but a solid, licking
odour, like fresh cut pine – or the breath
of a jersey snorting acetone in clouds
across a moonlit fence – something awkward
I couldn't quite embrace. But anyhows, it made
me cross, and I had a job to do.

On the slatted floor of the holding pen
a wether scraped its toes, long claws from
months in lucerne, away from limestone plains.
I leaned across the fence too long,
showed the beast the knife. I'd honed
it clean and bright on a wet stone –
that was why my mouth was dry:
I didn't know when she crossed the evening
shadows, or when she came into the shed.

The light would last another hour, the heat
would last all night. Not a night to kill,
but the beast had waited two days for this,
and it was now or turn it out. I could
smell her, sure, or was that some mirage
held warm in my head from half an hour
back when the Kroehns arrived by car.

I stared into the brown and yellow eyes
of the patient wether, and it stared into mine.
My hand could hold the knife quite still
though my chest and all my head was filled
with drumming sounds, with ratchet beats.

Her shadow fell, and then she rested
on the skun-pine rail nearby. I dropped
my eyes, released the beast. She wore
brown leather sandals, and a fine gold
chain about her ankle, and I quickly
looked away: I had a job to do.

I found a cord, tested well and greased
from many previous nights with beasts trapped
upon these boards. I firmly bound both forelegs
to a hind leg, and I let her see
the animal trussed upon the floor.

And while she gazed I lightly stropped the blade,
and from the corner of my eye I saw
how thick and wet her lips had grown, how red;
I saw the flicker of a vein
deep within her neck – and I saw her hair.

I whipped the knife into a post where it sang,
buried half an inch. And I
flung my shirt across the rail where Martha
waited. And, with the knife, I knelt upon
the shoulder of the beast, gripped its jaw

and I stretched the neck back tight. By now
her odour filled the air, calmed my charge,
and with a slight exaggeration, I paused,
then fed the blade across the throat, bore down,
brought panic to the head, the heart, and I
released life and blood in spurts,
and the sucking thing beneath my knee sang
pink, rattling gurgles – fierce, primitive songs
of death. Again the toes scratched messages
upon the boards, but everything that was
the beast pumped out across the slatted floor
and dripped into the dust. She stood calm,
her eyes afire. I cleaned

the blade upon my chest and leaned
against the fence. I boldly watched her now –
she turned her eyes to mine, and to the blood
dribbling on my flesh. Her hand reached out,
and she smeared the blood,
brushed it crudely with her palm.
Then she climbed across the rail into the pen.
I stooped beside the oozing throat
and dipped the killing knife into the blood.
I freed the cord and looped it handy in my belt.
Take off your shirt. My mouth could only whisper.
But when I turned and rose with clotting blood
spilling from the blade, her eyes still shone –
she shook her hair, stood ready to the waist.

Sheila, and Kevin – and me

A weeping tree gave me welcome night shade.
Blue powdery dark hung like thick smoke.
I stood unseen, waiting, blood keen,
behind the thin, leafy scrim.

            Her scented note, folded
deep in my pocket, gave my thumb
a sharp, certain edge – next week
her script would touch me again
with the minutes of loving to come.
And in the months to pass I might
show her page off, to Kevin, as thanks
for his courier task.

            She came like a cat
without noise on the lawn, though
her white wrap glowed like new snow.
She perched on a bench in the fern house,
just metres beyond where I leaned
on the peppercorn bough. I almost
called out a whisper, almost broke
from my hide, when a shadow came in
from the right. She stood, uncertain,
alarmed by the chuckle, the dry tenor
of Kevin – and they talked in murmurs
I found too low. Too low, too broken
for sense, but I thought more than once
they uttered my name.

I remained in the dark –
until he turned her to him – he kissed her
as I would have done. Did she reach
her fingers to play on his neck? – did
she shrug, uncoil calm, press close
to his chest, while his palms smoothed her
all over, slipped her back zipper down?
Were his chuckles answered with short,
pleasured words of the sort she would
murmur to me? Did they hear
my pulse race in curious anger
when he brushed her straps free
from her shoulder, took his lips
to the breasts, for kisses she had kept
all summer for me? Could I
say something, now, to stop this?

And she gasped, not surprised,
when his tongue turned to her ear,
heard his voice – say something bold?
She paused, almost stone in his arms.
But she thawed with his mouth
working soft on her own. And,
summer-stained skin to the waist,
she returned to the bench:
he moved closer, bent to kiss
her hair, and she did what
she'd not done for me.

Kevin
let her return first to the hall –
and before he set out – though
I could be mistaken – I thought
he smiled, and winked, at the night,
at the tree by the fernhouse, at me.

I passed half an hour, still
in the dark, and returned
to the dance without reading the note,
unsure – would the dawn confirm
how the summer should end? –
and with it my boyhood, tricked raw,
skinned by the loss of two friends?

Two with Bligh, from 28 April 1789

One

On board the *Bounty* sailors cheered –
we made no such fuss.

Two hundred warriors, small beside
their cane spears and palm tree curtain,
armed with eyes of blazing coal,
reeked of vengeance. We knew for certain

not all nineteen of us would live.
And it was Quartermaster Johnny Norton,
who wrestled with the coral-locked grapnel.
They grabbed and stoned him, and they fought on

though his pink head-flesh broke out
to take up ocean salt. He died
a pig's death and worse, pulped, bruised
too long past recognition. The screams they cried

rattled in my sleep these last seven years. But
at least I came home to England. My legs
swelled and grew sores, and my lungs and heart
shone clear beneath my fringe of ribs. We were the dregs

of sailors, even for the Admiralty, for whom
Johnny Norton died – he died without us.

Two

Puss on Bligh. My life
I owe to him, but his rusty
pride served him as a lash.
The way he spat his scorn
about the launch pumped
fear through men: hate sped along
their burnished arms, along the oars,
and it boiled the sea nearby.

Twelve days past, on Tofua
a seething herd brained John
Norton – all I could do was seize
my oar with fear, and pull, pull,
when Bligh tipped aboard. I would rather
it was Norton aboard, and Bligh
beneath the coral cudgels.
Still we scan the seascape
for a war canoe, heavy
with men who would eat us.

Birds. It hurts to part our lips,
though rain, not sun, sweeps everyday
across the bows. Dry biscuits, and
rain, sometimes half an ounce of pork.
And Miller made a snatch upon a booby,
sauced with blood, and boasting clear
and careless eyes – it had settled on the prow.
Bligh carved the carcass eighteen times
and mine was cold and blue and
gave up jelly, and it chewed and chewed.

We made passage to an island girded
by coral reefs. And we drank at springs,
and scraped oysters into toothless mouths.
Taggart wrestled the coxswain for a slip
of perch, then faced Bligh to dance
the nervous liar's gig before the dirk.
The red-eyed man Christian would have
drowned if we had not gathered
in a circle – he stoked the cutlass
into our noses and stirred our rotten breath
with the blade and hearty promises.
And we put to sea after
just one week on Sunday Island.

June 10th, and even Taggart sleeps
in the bilge, no flesh across his back,
and ulcers flaming from his thighs
to toes. We could not live on now –
bitter fun for our full complement of
eighteen men like empty oyster shells.
God alone knows how Taggart finds
the strength to leak from so many wounds.

I would die tonight, but I wait
to see Bligh stiffen too.

Land. Still worse – fires. We'll
gag the jaws of savages
even though we've strayed far
beyond Tahiti. Three bells –
too little light to know our end.
Too little … of, everything.

Fort Coupang's arrived, like
an albatross, and we're facing
butter and tea. But I mind, still,
I sit away from Bligh.

Mawson – 25 January 1912

Stainless cold, no scent, no ripple
in the steel blast, unnatural breath of ghosts
driven from Nimmis, screamed alive
days past but hard and solid now –
sharp and icy voices of a life.
You, haunting men – don't put out blame.
Your cold song rasps deep
between my riffled bones and useless skin – my
feet float in jelly ooze,
and loose souls pinch me enough
for all that came upon us.
Dog-lined, thin-headed too, wretched waste
claws up my chest, digs my throat black
with acid clampons. Never
will this be my life again, except
for you Nimmis, and for you, my Mertz.
I am flogged and peeled – ghosts, don't
play me into the crevasse, those thundering
steel mirrors fixed with ice slivers
set to knife me, don't
put me to grind between glassy pyramids,
cold, revengeful temples, where
minced men arm the blast with teeth.
Nimmis, Mertz, for you, for ghosts all
of us, give me on to men.

Yukon, 25 March 1962

(for Ralph and Helen – survivors)

What anger makes the cold,
the white shale frost,
the snow mallet
pounding cold,
the clockwork rasp
of coal-black frostbite?
Toes dead to the sole,
over-ripe, putrid, tethered
by singing pain, now still, now
twisting like the pellet
sometimes carried months
by rambling gut-shot moose.

One arm – and a soft zeppelin
loose beneath a parka,
a simmering bulbous limb
pinned by fear against ribs,
nibbled by two points of crushed bone
like brazen rodents,
worse since warm.

Conifers, ice, rocks – rock and snow
commanding everything: how
to save bones from wolves?
The ridiculous splinters
of the Howard monoplane.
A fire so mean it will not warm
itself. And the lisping quiet,
animal scuffles, slippery rabbits.

The special tree, chisel scored –
there, forty-eight – forty-nine
tomorrow. A jay yammering
indignant Morse, abruptly quiet –
startled, a droning fly,
a bitter sigh soon too tired
to breathe – a red ... balloon. A script.
Good morning. There are two other
planes on the way.

HMS *Megaera* at St Paul

Thrupp strung tents across the volcano
shell, where it slid into the ocean,
taking all St Paul down
to the fish. We'd flogged Percival
forty-eight with the cat;
he would only crouch and quiver,
blubbering while we stripped
sails, hammocks, oil, three
thousand pounds of biscuits,
and coal from the *Megaera*.

Three weeks had burst the Good Hope
pinhole into a flood beyond pumps.
We took St Paul from two Frenchies,
rats, goats, scores of penguins.
Thoms and me stood a sail boom
in a cairn, and we flew the ensign
upside down. Jones, an officer,
launched notes in bottles,
addressed to Australia, two months
east by barque. And inside a dark tent
I glimpsed wide-eyed M.F.
clutching a tobacco pouch,
sprawled upon a bench,
and I saw the bosun's mate.

Aye – what will men find here
when they find us here?

Wakefield Press

Friendly Street New Poets Two

Anna Brooks, Jenny Weight & David Cookson

*Cast off deliciously
into night ocean*

Delicious, provocative, uncompromising. Anna Brooks's
poetry speaks powerfully of sensuality, vulnerability, and
of delight in intimate meetings with nature.

*On the threshold we purchase
a nip of designer danger*

With wit and irony, Jenny Weight flies you beyond the
comfort zone into outer space then navigates the way back
to urban space. *A journey with attitude.*

*Your words rattle around me
like gravel on a roof*

You'll enjoy the sharp, satisfying impact of David Cookson's
images as he provides a lively and humorous commentary
on people and events. There's sensuality here too; tomatoes
never tasted so good.

ISBN 1 86254 374 7   RRP$14.95